THE ENTREPRENEUR'S COUNTDOWN WORKBOOK

Create Your Business in 7 Weeks

Copyright 2019 Numerical Insights LLC
Charlotte, NC, USA

All Rights Reserved
Printed in the United States of America

No part of this publication may be reproduced, stored in or introduced into a retrieval system, or transmitted, in any form, or by any means (electronic, mechanical, photocopying, recording or otherwise), without the prior permission of the publisher. Requests for permission should be directed to articles@numericalinsights.com.

This publication is intended for informational purposes only. Users of this guide are advised to do their own due diligence when it comes to making business decisions and all information, products and services that have been provided should be independently verified by your own qualified professionals. By reading this workbook, you agree that the author is not responsible for the success or failure of your business or investment decisions relating to any information presented in this workbook.

ISBN: 9781795700245

WHY THIS WORKBOOK?

The three biggest factors holding people back from starting a business are TIME, COST and FEAR.

TIME: You can work at your own pace. This workbook is designed for people who want to create their own business, under their own conditions, and without a large start-up cost. While we've set a planning timeline of 7 weeks, you can go as quickly or as slowly as you wish. The important thing is to move forward.

COST: We focus on low cost business start-ups. We'll focus on planning business launches that you can start from your home that don't require seeking out investors or spending thousands of dollars buying inventory or capital equipment.

FEAR: We take away the fear of business planning. We've "been there, done that." The author of this workbook launched her own business in 2013 and serves clients in multiple countries. This workbook captures the author's knowledge to save other entrepreneurs time, money and fear.

Contents

Introduction 1

Week 1: Finding Your First Idea 2

    How to Generate Your Idea 2

    Step 1: Preparation Questions 4

    Step 2: Business Topics 5

    Step 3: Idea Filters 7

    Step 4: Apply the Filters to Your Business Ideas 8

    Step 5: Idea Assessment 8

Week 2: Who Are My Customers 10

    Step 1: Am I a B2B or B2C Business? 12

    Step 2: Do My Customers Belong to Certain Groups? 13

    Step 3: Where Can I Reach My Customers? 13

Week 3: How Can I Reach My Customers and What Do I Tell Them? 16

    Step 1: What Should I Say to Customers? 17

    Step 2: Crafting Your Mission Statement 18

    Step 3: Crafting Your Customer Message for Ads and Social Media 19

Week 4: Should I Officially Register My Business? 23

Week 5: Don't Put Off Thinking About the Numbers! 25

    Spreadsheet or Accounting Program 26

    Desktop or Cloud 27

    Credit Cards and Bank Accounts 27

Week 6: Web Sites and Online Profiles 29

Week 7: Useful Business Tools 33

Launch Day! 36

Introduction

It's in us all... the desire to control our own destiny by owning a small business. But it's not always best to suddenly quit your job and risk it all in a new business venture. This workbook will help guide those of you looking to take only a small amount of risk to start a business.

Whether you're looking to create a business to replace your day job or to supplement your regular income, there are a lot of things you'll need to learn and, thankfully, a lot of great tools available to help you. In this workbook, we'll focus on businesses that you can start from your home that don't require seeking out investors or spending thousands of dollars buying inventory or capital equipment.

The three biggest factors holding back people from starting a business are TIME, COST and FEAR. We've created this workbook to help you get past the challenges of all three factors.

TIME
You can work at your own pace. We've set a planning timeline of 7 weeks, but you can go at your own speed. The important thing is to move forward.

COST
We focus on low cost business start-ups. We'll focus on planning business launches that you can start from your home without spending a lot of money.

FEAR
We take away the fear of business planning. We've "been there, done that." Having launched a successful business from nothing in 2013, We've put this workbook together to take away most of the fear and to save you a lot of time.

Week 1: Finding Your First Idea

Let's get started!

Generating ideas for your business is probably the toughest step that you will complete. For some people, the challenge is picking one idea from so many. For others, it's incredibly challenging to come up with the first idea.

How to Generate Your Idea

It is unlikely that you will sit down and suddenly come up with that one perfect idea. The following worksheet will help you jot down multiple ideas and show you how to filter through them using the idea funnel. Ideas that make it through the funnel are the ones with which you consider moving forward.

The activities in week 1 will require you to dedicate time to thinking through each step. You may also wish to discuss these activities with a friend or family member. For these reasons, it is best to dedicate multiple time slots on your calendar to completing the week 1 worksheet.

For your convenience, we have inserted a brief time planner for week 1 so you can record when you plan to dedicate time to completing the week 1 activities.

Week 1 Time Planner

Use the calendar below to record the time you will dedicate to work on the week 1 activities. Planning will help keep you on track.

Week Of:

Sunday

Monday

Tuesday

Wednesday

Thursday

Friday

Saturday

Now that you have scheduled time for your entrepreneur's countdown, return to this workbook at those times to begin working on this week's activities.

Step 1: Preparation Questions

Record your answers to the following questions.

What is it that you're passionate about or what makes you happy? Food? The arts? Technology? Or perhaps your passion is making money and you're flexible on the topic?

What is it that you're good at? These do not have to be items from the box above. You may be good at many things that don't excite you to the level that you would call them passions or say that they make you happy. Feel free to also ask friends and family what they think you're good at. Add these extra items in the box below.

Step 2: Business Topics

When you look at your responses to Step 1 (both tables above), what products or services can you offer related to those topics? You may need to do some research on products you can make or services you can provide that come from your responses in Step 1.

Generate a list of business topics and record them below.

	Business Topic	If this is from your passion list, place a check mark in this column.	If this is from your skills list, place a check mark in this column.
1			
2			
3			
4			
5			
6			
7			

For each of the business topics above, think about ways to generate **revenue** from those topics. Revenue is a source of income for your business. For example, will you generate income from selling products on eBay or Etsy?

- Can you sell your products or services directly to customers?
- If customers aren't likely to buy from you directly, can you generate passive income from affiliate revenue? (Affiliate programs pay a commission when customers of another company's product are referred by you. It's an income strategy of many bloggers and podcasters.)
- Can you build a large online or social following that would attract advertising revenue?

Generate a list of your revenue sources and record them below.

	Idea	Revenue Sources
1		
2		
3		
4		
5		
6		
7		

Copy your business ideas from the above table into the first column of the table shown on page 9. Only copy the ideas where you identified at least one revenue source.

Step 3: Idea Filters

In this section, record a list of conditions that each idea needs to meet in order to match your lifestyle preferences. Here are a few examples:

- If you plan to start a business while working full-time, perhaps your idea needs to accommodate your work schedule.
- Since this workbook is for people that want to create low-risk businesses, perhaps you need to specific your maximum business creation budget. What can you afford to spend to launch your business?
- Perhaps you're a stay-at-home mom that needs to restrict business activities to certain times during the day.
- Perhaps you are seeking the freedom to travel. Then one of your filters may be that you must be able to run your business from anywhere.

Think about the conditions under which your business idea must operate and record your filters below.

My business idea(s) must...

Filter #1	
Filter #2	
Filter #3	
Filter #4	
Filter #5	

Step 4: Apply the Filters to Your Business Ideas

For the ideas you copied into the table on page 9, which ones meet the conditions set by your filters? The ideas that make it through your filters are ideas that you are passionate about or skilled at, that have products or services that you think customers are willing to pay for and meet the conditions you need to be able to move forward.

Use the table on page 9 to apply your filters to your business ideas. If you need more space, feel free to create a spreadsheet or use a blank sheet of paper to create a larger table.

Ignore the column called **Idea Assessment** for now. We'll fill that in during Step 5.

Step 5: Idea Assessment

Which ideas made it through your filters? Take a look at your worksheet table and classify your ideas using the following categories. Record your classification in the **Ideas Assessment** column of the worksheet.

- **GO**: "I am willing to move forward with this idea."
- **NO GO**: "I definitely can't make this idea work under my conditions."
- **Modify / Rework**: "I have an idea that didn't make the GO list but I think I can rework it a bit to make it a GO."
- **HOLD**: "This is an idea that I can save for later because it might work better after I've completed one of the GO ideas."

Do you have multiple **GO** ideas? Or a few ideas that could be a **GO** if you modify or rework them?

We'll talk about reworking ideas next.

Idea #	Idea	Does it meet Filter #1?	Does it meet Filter #2?	Does it meet Filter #3?	Does it meet Filter #4?	Does it meet Filter #5?	Idea Assessment
	Description of idea						Go/NO GO
Example: 0		Yes	Yes	No	Yes	Yes	
1							
2							
3							
4							
5							
6							

Reworking Ideas

If you have an idea that needs to be reworked, think about what it would take to make that idea a **GO**.

- Is there are skill you think you're missing? Free classes for many skills can be found on sites like Coursera and EdX. Paid classes can be found on Udemy and Teachable.
- Is there something in your mind that holds the idea back? A lack of confidence? The fear of being successful?

In the box below, record the actions you need to take if you want to move a Modify/Rework idea to a **GO**. When you have completed that action, you can adjust that idea in the worksheet on page 9.

Review your final list of potential business ideas. If you didn't get any **GO** ideas or ideas that can be reworked to a GO, feel free to head back to Step 1 or 2 for some more creative thinking.

Rework Area

Example: I need to take an online podcasting course to move idea 4 to a GO. Course planned for February 7-14.

Week 2: Who Are My Customers

Week 2 Time Planner

Week Of:

Sunday

Monday

Tuesday

Wednesday

Thursday

Friday

Saturday

Now that you have scheduled time for your entrepreneur's countdown, return to this workbook at those times to begin working on this week's activities.

Follow the steps of this section to discover who your customers are and where you can reach them.

Step 1: Am I a B2B or B2C Business?

In the business world, customers come in two categories. If you sell your product or service to other businesses, you are B2B. This is just an abbreviation for "Business to Business." If you sell your product or service to individuals, you are B2C. This stands for "Business to Consumer."

Think about the products or services that you can offer in your business and determine which category of customers is likely to buy it. Don't feel as if you need to fill in all rows of this table. Most businesses launch with one product or service to offer since that's often a large project in itself. Additional products can be added later.

Record the name of your product or service in the first column. If you think it is a product that businesses will want to buy, answer YES to the B2B question in Column 2. If you think it is a product that individuals will buy, answer YES to the B2C question in Column 3.

Note: Some products and services can be sold to both customer groups, B2B and B2C.

Product / Service Name	Will You Sell it to Other Businesses (B2B)?	Will You Sell It Directly to Individuals (B2C)?

Step 2: Do My Customers Belong to Certain Groups?

Now that you know whether you are selling to companies, individuals or both, think about whether your customers are in certain groups.

For example, what you plan to offer may appeal more to men or women, people in a certain age group, income level, location, etc. These are called demographic groups.

Other products appeal to people regardless of their demographics. For example, your product may appeal to all ages and all genders but is most appealing to people with certain interests, passions, values or skills. Perhaps it appeals to groups with common characteristics like high-end home owners, small businesses or fans of a certain team or music group. These are called psychographics.

Think about your potential customers and list the customer groups to which you feel your product or services is most appealing. If you are still undecided about your business idea and have multiple ideas from Week 1, build a separate analysis for each idea.

Step 3: Where Can I Reach My Customers?

For each group you listed above, think about where you can reach them. Do they spend a lot of time online reading certain web sites? Do they prefer certain social media sites? Do they read certain magazines or attend certain conferences? Do they listen to particular podcasts?

It's difficult to keep up with the constantly changing media locations, so we've added a list of some of the popular media outlets at the end of this section to help you. If you don't need any help, just go ahead and fill out the chart below for your customer groups and where they get their information.

Group Name	Where do they get their information?

Media Outlets

Below is not an all-inclusive list and new locations are being added every day, but here are few places where your customers may "hang out." Choose the ones that align to your product type.

- Podcasts
- LinkedIn
- Facebook
- Twitter
- Industry magazines
- Radio
- Pinterest
- Reddit
- Quora
- Tumblr
- Etsy
- StumbleUpon
- Conferences
- Local business associations

How to Get It All Done

- Set goals and deadlines for yourself. Hold yourself accountable to finish your goals on time because you're the only person who can.
- Don't take on debt! We've all heard entrepreneurial stories of people putting $10,000 (that they don't have) on a credit card to gamble on the success of their business. While we hear of a few people that succeed this way, we don't hear of the thousands that don't. Remember, this workbook is about building something slowly and keeping the costs low. It's better to be financially responsible and patient than to be reckless.
- Be prepared to invest time and energy. It takes a lot to get started but it can be very rewarding. It gets easier later, once you have an established customer base.
- Focus. Don't get distracted by many different ideas. One entrepreneur called this the "bright, shiny object syndrome." Stick to your plan. Save extra ideas and prioritize them for the future.
- **Focus on creating value for customers first.** Revenue will follow. Building a business is more like a marathon, not a sprint. Focus on today. Broaden your offerings later.

Male and Female Entrepreneurs Think Differently

Why is this important? Decades of scientific studies have identified that men and women think differently when it comes to topics like confidence levels, the desire to take on higher level challenges and flexibility in working conditions. The author of this workbook has studied gender differences in several global corporations in addition to reviewing the scientific studies. The design of this workbook takes some of those differences into account.

This workbook intentionally provides the ability to plan an at-home business for stay-at-home moms or dads. Its focus is also on low-cost start-ups that working professionals can use to start, grow and transition out of the corporate world... or the recently unemployed that need a quick way to try to move forward.

This workbook is intentionally short and to-the-point, to allow readers to learn and plan quickly.

Week 3: How Can I Reach My Customers and What Do I Tell Them?

Week 3 Time Planner

Week Of:
Sunday
Monday
Tuesday
Wednesday
Thursday
Friday
Saturday

Step 1: What Should I Say to Customers?

In last week's template, you recorded where your potential customers could be reached, but we haven't determined what we want to say to them. Answer the following questions to help create your message.

What is it that you are offering to the market?

How much will it cost a customer to purchase your product or service?

What is the main benefit to the customer if they purchase it? How is this unique from what other companies may be offering, i.e. how will you stand out from similar businesses?

What are other benefits to the customer if they purchase it?

What would stop a customer from purchasing your offering? What will you say in your customer message to remove that objection or hesitation?

Why should your customer buy it today?

Step 2: Crafting Your Mission Statement

A mission statement is a quick way to say what you provide, to whom and why. It should not be more than 1-2 sentences. You can craft a quick mission statement using the following structure.

"We provide [*type of product or service*] to help [*customer group*] achieve [*benefit(s)*]."

As an example, let's look at the statement on the home page of a women's entrepreneurial site. It says:

"Company XYZ is where *women* come to *learn more about themselves...* and to *leverage that knowledge to become strong career professionals and entrepreneurs.*"

In the above statement, the customer group is "women." There are two benefits mentioned. The first is that women can "learn about themselves" and the second is that they can "leverage that knowledge to become strong career professionals and entrepreneurs."

It doesn't explicitly state any products or services, but since the first benefit is learning, what the site is offering is knowledge and information.

Now, it's your turn. Write your brief mission statement below.

Step 3: Crafting Your Customer Message for Ads and Social Media

Now that you have you mission statement, it's time to craft your customer message. How long or short this message is will depend on the places you post your message. For example, if you previously identified Twitter as a place to reach potential customers, you message needs to fit within 140 characters or you need to split your message across multiple tweets.

Facebook and LinkedIn will allow longer messages. However, you should create your messages to be clear, concise and to the point. Vey few people will read a long message. LinkedIn recently changed its feed algorithm to rank video posts higher than text posts.

If you plan to have a web site for your business, people tend to want more information there since they have come to your site to get enough information to feel comfortable about making a purchase from you. A future section of this workbook will help you decide whether you need a web site at the start of your business.

Refer to your previous worksheets to review the list of places you identified for finding customers. List them in the table on page 20 and write your customer message for each source. For some of them, you message can be the same. Feel free to include those in the same row of the table.

Some people like to mention prices in their customer message if they feel that will attract people. Others prefer to focus on the benefits in order to get customers to click a link to direct them to where the product/service can be purchased or where more information can be found.

In either case, messages should refer to benefits for the customer and should somehow tell the customer why this offering is unique from what others offer. How will it help them?

If you need more space, feel free to write your table on a separate sheet of paper or in a spreadsheet.

Where will this message be posted?	What will the message say? Include a link of where to make a purchase or where to find more information.

Final Comments for Week 3

Up to this point, you should have spent absolutely nothing on this business. The first three weeks of work have been about thinking and planning. In future weeks, this workbook will guide you through a few decisions of what to buy before your official business launch.

> Working hard for something you don't love is called stress.
>
> Working hard for something you do love is called passion.

The Laws of Attraction: Getting Customers to Come to You

One of the first challenges in your business is attracting customers to your product or service. As you begin to think about marketing your business and building your brand, realize that it will be a series of activities spread across various marketing channels. Be patient. If you have just launched your business, it will take time to build up and attract an audience. People will have to see your company name often enough that the brand becomes familiar. People generally trust a brand more if they are repeatedly exposed to it.

Pulling Customers Toward You

When I first read a book on the topic of consulting, it introduced me to a term called "marketing gravity." Typical sales activities have the sales person reaching out to potential clients. With "marketing gravity" activities, you are building your brand with activities which may bring clients to you. Having them come to you is much less work that you trying to find them.

Here are a few ways to start building your brand to increase your "customer attraction."

Writing Articles and Blogs

Writing articles is a great way to demonstrate that you are knowledgeable about your products and services. Ideally, you want to post your articles in places where you potential customers "hang out." Initially, it may be difficult to get your article into industry magazines or popular business magazines, so begin with places like your LinkedIn blog and your own web site or Facebook page.

Initially, blogs on your own web site will not have a large audience. Definitely post on your own site to start building that audience and improving your SEO ranking, but also try to find places willing to let you guest blog. Guest blogging means that your article is posted on someone else's web site so try to select locations where your potential customers visit and ensure that the site will link back to your own site or your LinkedIn / Facebook page.

eBooks

eBooks are another great way to attract potential customers. These don't have to be full-length books as people have become used to seeing short eBooks given away for free on company web sites. The key here is to create an eBook on a subject that relates to your business and that potential customers will find useful. The value in producing an eBook is that you can require that potential customers sign up for your email list in order to get the book for free. This builds your email list audience and allows you to market to them later.

YouTube

Did you know that YouTube is the second-most popular search engine behind Google? That's probably no surprise given that Google owns them. That makes YouTube an excellent place to attract an audience if you know or are willing to learn how to make video files.

Week 4: Should I Officially Register My Business?

Week 4 Time Planner

Week Of:

Sunday

Monday

Tuesday

Wednesday

Thursday

Friday

Saturday

This week is about deciding what type of business entity you will be... or whether you'll be an officially registered business at all.

Some businesses operate as sole proprietors. This means that the business and the person are one and the same in the eyes of the law. The risk with this business arrangement is that if anyone decides to file a lawsuit against your company, they can go after your personal assets (house, car, savings accounts, etc.)

This is why many people decide to officially register their business. In both the USA and Canada, the greatest level of protection is if you register as a corporation. Under this arrangement, you will file tax returns for the business and you would also file personal tax returns. Legally, you and the business are two different entities. Any lawsuit brought against your company can only go after the assets that are in the business, not your personal assets.

If you're in the USA, there is another option and it's the option that most small businesses choose. This option is called LLC which stands for Limited Liability Corporation. The cost of becoming an LLC is lower than the cost of being a corporation. Also, as an LLC, your business income flows onto your personal tax return so you don't have to file a separate tax return for your business.

This is the most popular option for small businesses since it costs less than becoming a corporation, requires less administrative obligations, but still provides the business owner with liability protection. As a business grows, eventually there's a revenue level where it makes sense to become a corporation.

Most government locations have a web site where you can file an online form to create your business, register your business name and pay the fee. If you are in the USA, search for the government site for your home state.

If you aren't comfortable with filing the paperwork yourself but would like to avoid the expenses of hiring a lawyer, there are services out there such as LegalZoom.

I'm not a legal expert, so I recommend reading more about the different business types before making a decision. If you have a larger budget, feel free to speak with a lawyer and accountant.

Week 5: Don't Put Off Thinking About the Numbers!

Week 5 Time Planner

Week Of:

Sunday

Monday

Tuesday

Wednesday

Thursday

Friday

Saturday

If you decided to register your business as an LLC or Corporation, then congratulations! You officially have a business name. If you've decided to operate as a sole proprietor, then you will operate under your own name.

Either way, it's now time to think about how you will keep track of your business. As you spend money on your business, you will need to record your expenses. As you start to sell products and services to clients, you will need to record revenue.

Whatever you do, don't ignore the financial side of your business. It is crucial to know where your business stands financially, every day. Don't collect receipts and put them in a shoe box unseen until the end of the year! Most businesses fail because of cash flow issues, not a lack of sales.

Spreadsheet or Accounting Program

It is possible to track your expenses using a spreadsheet program like Microsoft Excel or Google Sheets. This is okay if you have very few transactions to record. However, as you grow, this will take more of your time and is more prone to errors.

If you prefer to spend your time on your business rather than in a spreadsheet, an accounting program can save you a lot of time. The product I have used for 15 years is QuickBooks Desktop Pro. Here's how QuickBooks helps you.

- Entering expenses is as simple as clicking on an icon that says, "Enter Bills." Enter the vendor name, the amount, and the type of item you purchased.
- Creating invoices is also simple. Click on an icon that says, "Create Invoices." Enter the client information or select from an existing client list. Enter details of what they received from you and the cost. If their profile has an email address, you can even send the invoice from inside QuickBooks.
- The program will track the due date of all invoices and create a reminder for you to check with a client when their payment is late.

You can also divide what you sell into classes inside QuickBooks to see which products/services are the most profitable for your business. This helps you with future decisions about which products to keep selling and which ones to retire.

Desktop or Cloud

The desktop version is preferred by those who don't want their business data stored in the cloud. However, if the type of business you have means you are rarely in your office, like a lawn mowing or house cleaning service, you may prefer the cloud version to be able to access it on-the-go. As with all software these days, vendors are moving everyone to cloud versions that are easier to maintain.

Credit Cards and Bank Accounts

If you registered your business as an LLC or Corporation, it is very important to set up a separate bank account and credit card for your business. This separates your business transactions from your personal transactions.

Why is this separation crucial? If someone files a lawsuit against your business and you have been using your personal bank account and credit card for your business, then they can argue that you and the business are the same thing. At that point, you are risking your personal assets. If you keep business and personal transactions clearly separate, then your liability protection is more likely to help you shield your personal assets.

If you did not register your business, it is still a good idea to have a separate credit card from your personal card so you can easily track what you are spending to run your sole proprietorship.

Use the table on the following page to record the decisions you made this week.

Business Question	Decision
What tool will I use to track my income and expenses?	
Do I need to get a credit card for my business?	
Do I need to set up a bank account for my business?	

We've provided a short to-do list for you to record items to need to do related to the decisions above.

To Do List

Week 6: Web Sites and Online Profiles

Week 6 Time Planner

Week Of:

Sunday

Monday

Tuesday

Wednesday

Thursday

Friday

Saturday

By now, you've put a great deal of thought into your business: the products or services you will offer, what you will say to customers, whether you will register yourself as a certain legal business type.

This week's decision will be a lot easier to make as we discuss the following question:

Do I Need a Web Site?

Whether you need a web site will depend on what you're selling and where you plan to sell it. Answering this question is easiest if we provide a few examples. Remember that we are approaching our business launches from a low-risk point of view. That means that we would like to remain a low-cost business for as long as possible.

If you plan to be an independent consultant, then you can initially operate your online presence from a LinkedIn profile page. LinkedIn provides enough detail that you can provide prospective clients with details about your services, your educational background and any projects you've conducted in the past. Eventually, you will want to have your own web site where you can provide more information and control the way your services are presented. However, if you'd like to avoid that cost for a while, you can hold off on building a company web site until you land that first client and get paid. If you have the luxury of being able to use some spare money you've saved up, then go ahead and build your site.

If you plan to sell products online, then the best way to start selling is to put a few items for sale on popular sites such as eBay or Etsy. For a low risk business launch, what you're looking for is places to list your items for sale where there is no fee to pay unless your product sells. Like the consultant example, you may eventually want to create your own e-commerce site, but in the beginning, it's best to use sites that already have a large amount of traffic. Building your own site means that you will also spend a lot of time trying to drive traffic to your site. Remember to ask yourself, "Where are my customers going to look first if they want the item I'm selling?"

Think about your own business and decide which of the options below is best for you:

- I won't need to build a web site.
- I don't need a web site now, but I will in the future.
- I definitely need a web site sooner rather than later.

Circle one of the above options to record your decision.

Completing Your Online Profile

During this week, you will also want to set up other areas of your social profile. Here are several items to set up if you previously identified these as a place where your customers are likely to be.

1. A Facebook page: Is your business one where people are likely to look on Facebook to find you?
2. Will people seek to interact with your business on Twitter?
3. Are people likely to look you up on LinkedIn to confirm the validity of your business?

Make a list of the social media locations that make sense for your business and set up business accounts for those sites. Make sure you pick ID/profile names that match your business name as closely as possible.

If you decided that you definitely need a web site for your business, try to make your web site and social accounts all look similar in terms of branding (use the same logo, same color scheme, etc.).

We've included a table on the next page for you to record your list of online locations, along with their user ID and password.

Online Locations and Sign-in Information

Online Location	User ID	Password

Our future growth relies on competitiveness and innovation.

Be the growth. Be the innovation.

Week 7: Useful Business Tools

Week 7 Time Planner

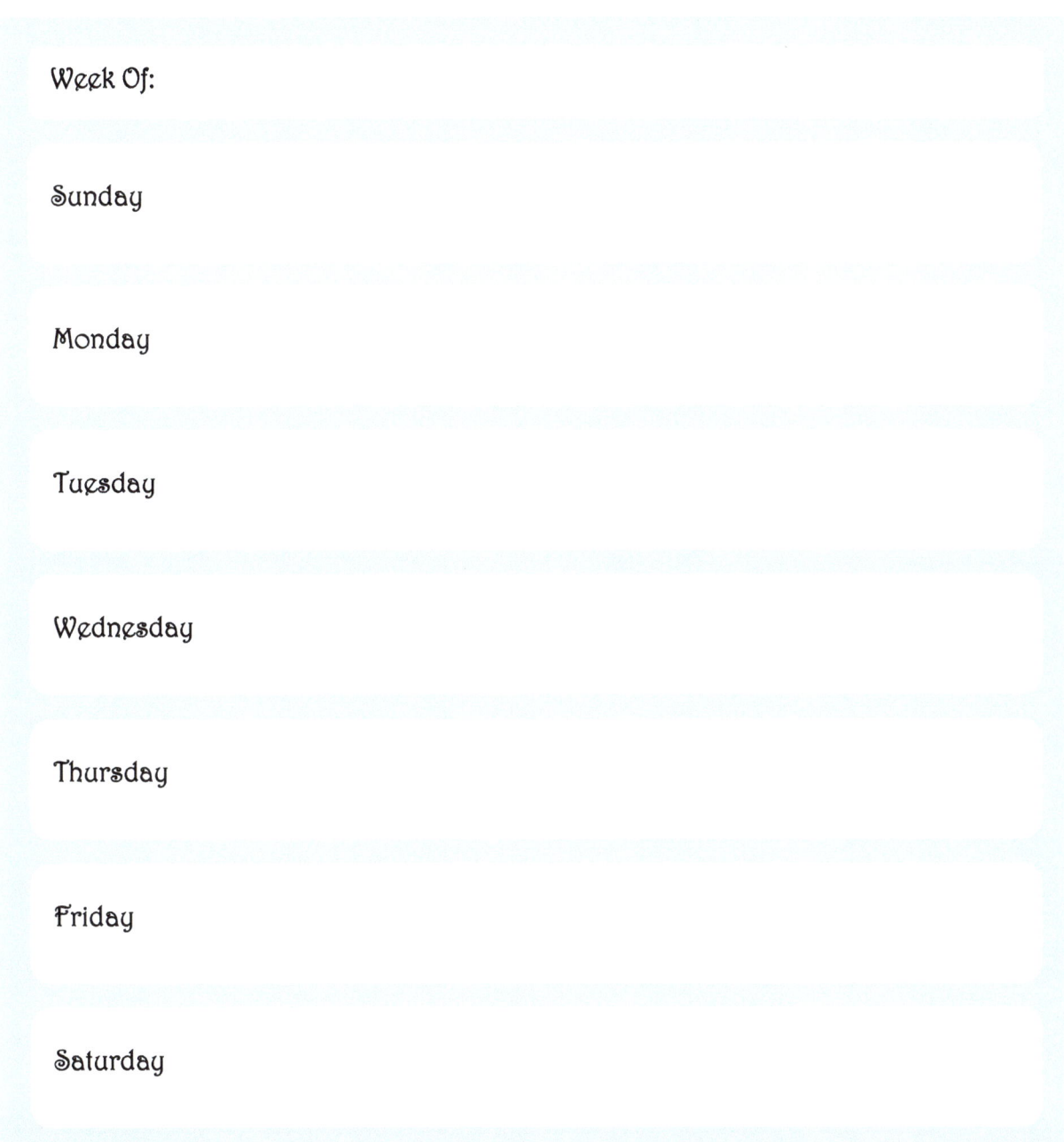

Week Of:

Sunday

Monday

Tuesday

Wednesday

Thursday

Friday

Saturday

Now that you have scheduled time for your entrepreneur's countdown, return to this workbook at those times to begin working on this week's activities.

By now, you've been very busy and you could use a week to catch up on a long list of To Do items that you set for yourself. So, this week, we'll provide information on tools that might be useful in your business. Not all tools will apply to all business types and for some categories, multiple tools are available. I'll also answer some common questions. Use your time this week to catch up on incomplete To Do items and to research the tools below that you think might be useful.

Tools

There are more options for these categories than are listed below. The table shows the ones that are most popular at the time of creating this workbook.

Category	Tool Name
Team collaboration	Microsoft Teams (part of Office 365), Slack
Webcasting	Microsoft Skype for Business (part of Office 365), Zoom, Go To Meeting
Phone number (..because it's best not to give out your person number.)	Skype, Google Voice
Podcast hosting	Libsyn, Buzzsprout
Web sites	Squarespace, WordPress, WIX
Social media productivity	Hootsuite: allows you to post to multiple social media places at once.

Do I Really Need Business Cards?

This is a frequent question received from individuals trying to start a business. While business cards are not expensive, they are an added cost to your business. Some businesses need them. Some don't.

If you plan to attend a lot of networking meetings, then business cards are a must. If you have a product that you plan to take to local shows to sell, then make sure you bring business cards or a brochure with you. People that don't buy your product immediately, will still have an easy way to find you and your web site and may make a purchase later.

If you plan to be an online blogger or podcaster where most of your customer interaction is online, then you can probably skip the cost of business cards initially. You can always order them later if you find yourself being invited to speak at a conference or local event.

So, for your own business, think about where you plan to go to find your customers and decide whether you need to order business cards for the start of your business. Record your decision below by circling it.

- I need business cards for the start of my business.
- I don't need them for the start of my business.

To organize Week 7, the following table is provided for you to list what you need to do this week in relation to tools and business cards.

Activity	Completed (Y/N)

Launch Day!

Today is the day you launch your business (if you haven't already!).

In the past 7 weeks, you've worked hard to:

1. Generate ideas for your business and use your own criteria to pick a business that meets your lifestyle preferences.
2. Identify your customers and customer groups.
3. Craft your vision statement and your customer message.
4. Determine which type of business entity you will be.
5. Learn the importance of tracking business expenses and income.
6. Create your initial online presence.
7. Learn about some of the useful tools available to make running your business easier.

And now, you're ready!

It's time to let everyone know that you're in business and show them what you have to offer.

Here are a few final words of advice:

- Tell everyone you know about your business. You may think that the person you're telling can't help you in any way, but you never know who they might know. Use the table on page 35 to record who you need to tell and how you will tell them. Will you send them an email? Telephone them? Tell them in person?
- Get as much free marketing exposure as you can. Offer to post a guest blog on a web site that has the audience you'd like to reach. Answer questions on an expert web site.
- Set aside a few minutes each day to post short messages to your social media accounts. Depending on the ones you've chosen to use for your business, there are some free tools out there to help you post to more than one at the same time. See the tools list in Week 7 of this workbook.

Who I Need to Tell	How I Will Tell Them (Email, Phone, In Person)

And finally, **let me know that you launched your business!**

Go to www.HERpreneurs.com and click on the word, **CONTACT**, from the main menu. Use the online form to tell me about you and your new business.

You may also want to bookmark the entrepreneur's resources page on the web site above. We update that page as new and useful tools are discovered.

Happy Launch Day!